GALAXY S24 VS IPHONE 14 SERIES

A Tale Of Two Tech Titans and the Clash Of Innovations

Nathaniel Tuner

Table of contents

OVERVIEW

The launch of the Galaxy S24 marks a pivotal moment for Samsung, as it unveils its latest flagship smartphone to the world. This event is not just about the release of a new device but signifies Samsung's commitment to pushing the boundaries of mobile technology. As one of the leading players in the smartphone industry, Samsung consistently seeks to redefine user experiences, and the Galaxy S24 is anticipated to be a testament to this commitment.

The Galaxy S24 launch is expected to draw significant attention due to its role in shaping Samsung's smartphone lineup. In the ever-evolving landscape of mobile technology, each flagship release contributes to the brand's identity and influences industry trends. The S24, with its rumored features and innovations, is poised to be a cornerstone in Samsung's portfolio, showcasing the company's prowess in design, technology, and user-centric advancements.

Simultaneously, it's crucial to acknowledge the broader context within which the Galaxy S24 emerges – the competitive field of flagship smartphones. In this context, the Galaxy S24 isn't just a singular device but a strategic move by Samsung to maintain its position and relevance in the highly dynamic market.

As we delve into the Galaxy S24, it's essential to set the stage by considering another major player in the smartphone arena – the Apple iPhone 14 Series. Apple's iPhone releases have consistently set industry standards and captured the imagination of users worldwide. The juxtaposition of the Galaxy S24 and the iPhone 14 Series introduces an intriguing narrative of technological innovation, design philosophies, and the perpetual competition for market supremacy.

Significance of Galaxy S24 in Samsung's Lineup

The Galaxy S24 holds immense significance within Samsung's extensive lineup of smartphones. Samsung's S series has been the torchbearer of innovation and technological advancements, often setting the tone for the industry. The S24, being the latest iteration, is expected to build upon the legacy of its predecessors while introducing novel features that cater to the evolving needs of consumers.

One of the key aspects of the Galaxy S24's significance lies in its role as a trendsetter. Samsung has a history of introducing cutting-edge technologies through its flagship devices, and the S24 is anticipated to be no different. Whether it's advancements in camera capabilities, display technology, or AI integration, the S24 is expected to showcase Samsung's vision for the future of smartphones.

Moreover, the success of the Galaxy S24 is critical for Samsung's market positioning. In an era where competition is fierce, a flagship device not only serves as a revenue generator but also as a brand ambassador. Positive reception and strong sales of the S24 can elevate Samsung's brand image, reinforcing its position as an industry leader.

Introduction to Apple iPhone 14 Series

On the other side of the spectrum, Apple's iPhone 14 Series emerges as a highly anticipated release in the tech world. Apple, known for its meticulous design philosophy and seamless integration of hardware and software, consistently delivers products that resonate with a global audience. The iPhone 14 Series is expected to continue this tradition while introducing innovations that align with Apple's commitment to excellence.

The introduction of the iPhone 14 Series is not just about unveiling new smartphones; it's a reflection of Apple's strategy to stay ahead in a competitive market. Apple's ability to set trends, influence consumer preferences, and maintain a dedicated user base positions the iPhone 14 Series as a key player in shaping the smartphone landscape in the coming years.

The iPhone 14 Series is likely to showcase advancements in processing power, camera technology, and software capabilities. As Apple strives to provide a seamless ecosystem across its devices, the iPhone 14 Series becomes a central element in this interconnected web of Apple products.

In conclusion, the introduction of the Galaxy S24 and the Apple iPhone 14 Series sets the stage for a captivating exploration into the latest advancements in mobile technology. These flagship releases not only represent the pinnacle of their respective brands but also contribute to the ongoing narrative of innovation and competition within the smartphone industry. As we delve deeper into the features, design elements, and market strategies of these devices, a clearer picture will emerge of the direction in which the smartphone landscape is headed.

GALAXY S24 MODELS: A Comprehensive Exploration

The Galaxy S24 lineup, comprising the standard S24, the larger S24 Plus, and the pinnacle of Samsung's innovation, the S24 Ultra, represents the culmination of years of technological advancement and consumer-centric design. Each model within this series is crafted to cater to distinct preferences, offering a range of features that appeal to a broad spectrum of users.

1. Detailed Look at S24, S24 Plus, and S24 Ultra

1.1 Galaxy S24:

The standard S24 is poised to be the embodiment of Samsung's commitment to providing a flagship experience for a wide audience. With a well-balanced form factor and cutting-edge technology, the S24 is expected to cater to users who prioritize a comfortable grip without compromising on performance. The model is likely to feature the latest Qualcomm Snapdragon 8 Gen 3 processor, ensuring seamless multitasking and efficient performance for day-to-day activities.

The camera setup on the S24 is anticipated to showcase improvements in zoom quality, enhancing the user's photography experience. Samsung's dedication to refining camera technology across its lineup positions the S24 as a reliable choice for photography enthusiasts.

1.2 Galaxy S24 Plus:

Building upon the foundation laid by the S24, the S24 Plus aims to deliver an enhanced experience for users seeking a larger display and additional features. The "Plus" variant traditionally offers a larger screen size, catering to those who prioritize a more immersive viewing experience. The S24 Plus is expected to share many specifications with its standard counterpart, including the advanced Snapdragon 8 Gen 3 processor and improvements in camera technology.

The S24 Plus could potentially differentiate itself through additional battery optimizations, ensuring extended usage without compromising on performance. This model is designed for users who value a balance between a spacious display, powerful performance, and an extended battery life.

1.3 Galaxy S24 Ultra:

At the apex of the Galaxy S24 lineup stands the S24 Ultra, a device that embodies Samsung's technological prowess and commitment to pushing the boundaries of innovation. Anticipated to feature a titanium frame, the S24 Ultra aims to set new standards in terms of build quality and durability. The titanium construction not only adds a premium touch but also contributes to the device's robustness.

The S24 Ultra is expected to boast an advanced camera system, possibly incorporating groundbreaking features to elevate the photography and videography experience. Samsung's focus on providing a comprehensive mobile AI experience, as seen with the release of Gauss, may manifest in unique AI-driven capabilities on the S24 Ultra, further differentiating it from other models in the lineup.

2. Key Features and Differentiators

2.1 Processor Power and Performance:

A shared feature across the S24 lineup is the utilization of the Qualcomm Snapdragon 8 Gen 3 processor, highlighting Samsung's commitment to delivering cutting-edge performance. This processor, known for its efficiency and power, ensures that users across all models experience smooth navigation, fast app launches, and responsive multitasking.

2.2 Camera Innovations:

The camera systems on the Galaxy S24 models are a focal point of differentiation. While all models are expected to see improvements in zoom quality, the S24 Ultra is likely to lead the pack with an advanced camera setup, possibly incorporating larger sensors and innovative features.

Samsung's dedication to photography is evident in its continuous efforts to redefine smartphone imaging capabilities.

2.3 Display Technology:

Each model in the S24 lineup is anticipated to feature a vibrant and immersive display, showcasing Samsung's expertise in screen technology. The standard S24 and S24 Plus are expected to offer excellent viewing experiences, while the S24 Ultra might take it a step further with potentially larger and more advanced display technology.

2.4 Battery Life and Optimization:

Differences in battery life are likely to be a key factor in distinguishing between the models. The S24 Ultra, with its larger form factor, may house a substantial battery, potentially providing extended usage between charges. Samsung's focus on battery optimization across the lineup ensures that users can rely on their devices throughout the day.

2.5 Design Elements:

The design philosophy of each model contributes to its distinct identity. The standard S24, with its balanced form factor, appeals to users seeking a compact yet powerful device. The S24 Plus, with its larger screen, caters to those who prioritize a more extensive display for multimedia consumption.

The S24 Ultra, with its titanium frame, sets itself apart as a premium flagship device.

In conclusion, the Galaxy S24 lineup offers a diverse array of models, each catering to specific user preferences and priorities. Whether one prioritizes a compact design, an immersive display, or cutting-edge camera technology, the S24 series aims to provide a tailored experience. As Samsung continues to push the boundaries of innovation, the Galaxy S24 lineup stands as a testament to the brand's commitment to delivering excellence in the world of smartphones.

APPLE IPHONE 14 SERIES: REDEFINING EXCELLENCE

1. Overview of iPhone 14, iPhone 14 Pro, and iPhone 14 Pro Max

The iPhone 14 Series, Apple's latest venture into the realm of smartphones, promises to be a testament to the company's dedication to innovation and user-centric design. Comprising the iPhone 14, iPhone 14 Pro, and iPhone 14 Pro Max, this series aims to build upon the success of its predecessors while introducing a host of new features and improvements.

1.1 iPhone 14:

The standard iPhone 14, likely to be the cornerstone of the series, is expected to embody Apple's core principles of simplicity, elegance, and functionality. With a focus on providing a seamless user experience, the iPhone 14 is anticipated to feature a sleek design, an advanced A16 chipset for enhanced performance, and improvements in camera technology. This model is likely to appeal to a broad audience, offering a perfect blend of form and function.

1.2 iPhone 14 Pro:

The iPhone 14 Pro, positioned as a more advanced variant, is expected to cater to users who demand cutting-edge technology and premium features. Building upon the foundation of the standard model, the iPhone 14 Pro is likely to introduce a ProMotion display with a higher refresh rate for smoother animations and responsiveness. Additionally, it may incorporate advanced camera capabilities, catering to photography enthusiasts and professionals seeking a versatile and powerful imaging tool.

1.3 iPhone 14 Pro Max:

At the zenith of the iPhone 14 Series stands the Pro Max variant, aimed at delivering the most comprehensive and advanced smartphone experience. The Pro Max is expected to feature a larger display, possibly incorporating the latest display technology for vivid colors and increased brightness. With a focus on maximizing performance and user satisfaction, the Pro Max is likely to boast an expansive battery, ensuring prolonged usage without compromise.

2. Notable Features and Innovations

2.1 Advanced A16 Chipset:

A highlight of the iPhone 14 Series is the introduction of the A16 chipset, Apple's latest iteration of its custom-designed processors. Known for their efficiency and performance, Apple's chipsets set the standard for mobile processing power. The A16 is expected to bring notable improvements in speed, graphics performance, and energy efficiency, contributing to an overall enhanced user experience across all iPhone 14 models.

2.2 ProMotion Display Technology:

The ProMotion display, likely to debut with the iPhone 14 Pro and Pro Max, is anticipated to offer a higher refresh rate, possibly up to 120Hz or beyond. This innovation enhances the overall visual experience by providing smoother scrolling, more responsive touch interactions, and improved fluidity in animations. The ProMotion technology is poised to elevate the display quality, making it a standout feature for users who prioritize an immersive visual experience.

2.3 Camera Innovations:

Apple's focus on photography has been a consistent theme, and the iPhone 14 Series is expected to further advance camera technology. The Pro and Pro Max models might introduce improvements in low-light photography, enhanced optical zoom capabilities, and possibly new features aimed at pushing the boundaries of smartphone imaging. These innovations cater to users who consider camera performance a crucial aspect of their smartphone usage.

2.4 Enhanced Battery Life:

With each new iPhone iteration, Apple places emphasis on optimizing battery life. The iPhone 14 Series is anticipated to continue this trend, possibly introducing advancements in battery technology or optimization strategies. The Pro Max variant, with its larger form factor, may house a substantial battery, ensuring users can rely on their devices throughout the day without the need for frequent charging.

2.5 Design Philosophy:

Apple's design philosophy has always been characterized by elegance and simplicity. The iPhone 14 Series is expected to adhere to these principles while possibly introducing subtle design refinements. The use of premium materials and meticulous attention to detail in crafting the device is likely to contribute to its overall aesthetic appeal.

2.6 Software Enhancements:

The iPhone 14 Series will likely debut with the latest iteration of iOS, introducing new features and optimizations. Apple's commitment to providing a seamless ecosystem across its devices ensures that users can enjoy a cohesive and integrated experience, from the iPhone to other Apple products.

2.7 Connectivity and 5G Integration:

As technology evolves, so does connectivity. The iPhone 14 Series is anticipated to feature advanced 5G capabilities, ensuring faster download and upload speeds, low latency, and an overall improved internet experience. This is particularly relevant in a world where connectivity plays a crucial role in daily tasks and activities.

In conclusion, the iPhone 14 Series stands as a testament to Apple's unwavering commitment to delivering excellence in the smartphone industry. With a range of models catering to diverse user preferences and needs, the series is poised to set new standards in performance, design, and innovation. As we eagerly anticipate the official unveiling, it's clear that the iPhone 14 Series will play a significant role in shaping the future of smartphones and solidifying Apple's position at the forefront of technological advancement.

Design and Build: Galaxy S24

The design and build of a smartphone are critical elements that not only contribute to the device's aesthetics but also impact its durability, ergonomics, and overall user experience. In the case of the Galaxy S24, Samsung continues its legacy of combining form and function to create a device that is not only visually appealing but also practical and robust.

Materials Used in Galaxy S24

1. Titanium Frame:

One of the standout features in the Galaxy S24 is the incorporation of a titanium frame in the S24 Ultra variant. Titanium is renowned for its exceptional strength-to-weight ratio, making it an ideal material for a smartphone frame. Not only does it lend a premium feel to the device, but it also enhances its structural integrity, providing durability and resistance to external stresses. This move reflects Samsung's commitment to pushing the boundaries of material innovation in smartphone construction.

2. Glass Back Panel:

The Galaxy S24 is expected to maintain the tradition of a glass back panel, contributing to its sleek and modern design. Glass not only adds a premium touch but also facilitates wireless charging, a feature that has become increasingly standard in flagship smartphones. The choice of glass aligns with Samsung's focus on creating devices that are not only technologically advanced but also visually appealing and comfortable to hold.

3. Aluminum or Glass Frame:

While the S24 Ultra boasts a titanium frame, the standard S24 and S24 Plus models may opt for materials like aluminum or a reinforced glass frame. These materials strike a balance between durability and weight, contributing to a device that is both sturdy and manageable in terms of size and weight. The choice of materials across the lineup reflects Samsung's consideration of diverse user preferences.

4. Display Technology:

The design of the Galaxy S24 extends to its display technology. Samsung, known for its expertise in producing vibrant and high-quality displays, is expected to feature an AMOLED display in the S24 series. This not only ensures rich and immersive visuals but also contributes to the overall design aesthetic by allowing for curved edges and minimal bezels.

5. Water and Dust Resistance:

Samsung has consistently incorporated water and dust resistance in its flagship devices, and the Galaxy S24 is likely to continue this trend. The use of gaskets, seals, and protective coatings on internal components ensures that the device can withstand exposure to water and dust, enhancing its durability and longevity.

Design and Build: Apple iPhone 14 Series

Apple's design philosophy is synonymous with simplicity, elegance, and meticulous attention to detail. The iPhone 14 Series is poised to embody these principles while introducing refinements and innovations that contribute to a cohesive and visually stunning device.

Design Elements in Apple iPhone 14 Series

1. Premium Materials:

Apple is known for its use of premium materials, and the iPhone 14 Series is expected to follow suit. The choice of materials plays a crucial role in both the aesthetics and durability of the device. Historically, Apple has favored materials like glass and aluminum, which not only lend a premium feel but also facilitate wireless charging.

2. Ceramic Shield:

The iPhone 14 Series may continue to feature the Ceramic Shield front cover, introduced in previous models. This material, developed in collaboration with Corning, is known for its durability and enhanced drop performance. It adds an extra layer of protection to the display, contributing to the overall robustness of the device.

3. Aluminum or Stainless Steel Frame:

Apple typically employs aluminum for the frame in standard models and stainless steel for the Pro variants. This choice not only differentiates between models but also reflects Apple's attention to detail. Aluminum offers a lightweight yet durable option, while stainless steel provides a more premium and robust feel.

4. All-Screen Design:

Apple's commitment to an all-screen design, minimizing bezels and maximizing the display area, is expected to continue with the iPhone 14 Series. This design element not only enhances the visual appeal but also contributes to a more immersive user experience. The removal of physical buttons and the integration of Face ID technology also contribute to the clean and streamlined design.

5. ProMotion Display:

The Pro models in the iPhone 14 Series are likely to feature the ProMotion display with a higher refresh rate, contributing to smoother animations and improved responsiveness. This design innovation enhances the overall user experience, especially for users who prioritize fluid interactions and visuals.

6. Precision Engineering:

Apple is known for its precision engineering, and this is evident in the meticulous construction of each iPhone. From the alignment of buttons to the placement of speakers, every detail is carefully considered. This commitment to precision engineering not only ensures a device that is aesthetically pleasing but also contributes to its functionality and ease of use.

7. Sustainability Initiatives:

In recent years, Apple has increasingly focused on sustainability in its product design. The iPhone 14 Series may feature recycled and responsibly sourced materials, aligning with Apple's commitment to reducing its environmental impact. This aspect of design reflects a broader awareness of the importance of sustainability in the tech industry.

In conclusion, both the Galaxy S24 and the iPhone 14 Series exemplify the commitment of Samsung and Apple, respectively, to create smartphones that seamlessly integrate cutting-edge technology with visually appealing and durable design. The choice of materials, attention to detail, and consideration of user experience contribute to devices that not only meet the functional needs of users but also resonate on a sensory and aesthetic level. The design and build of these flagship smartphones set the stage for a new era in mobile technology, where innovation and craftsmanship converge to create devices that transcend mere utility.

PROCESSING POWER: GALAXY S24

The processing power of a smartphone is a critical factor in determining its overall performance, from swift app launches to seamless multitasking. The Galaxy S24, Samsung's flagship smartphone, is anticipated to feature the Qualcomm Snapdragon 8 Gen 3, a chipset designed to deliver cutting-edge performance and efficiency.

Qualcomm Snapdragon 8 Gen 3 in Galaxy S24

1. Technological Advancements:

The Qualcomm Snapdragon 8 Gen 3 represents the pinnacle of Qualcomm's mobile processor technology. It is built on the latest advancements in semiconductor manufacturing, likely leveraging a 5nm or more advanced process node. This results in a chip that is not only powerful but also energy-efficient, contributing to improved battery life and overall device longevity.

2. CPU Architecture:

The Galaxy S24's processing power is driven by the CPU architecture embedded in the Snapdragon 8 Gen 3. Details about the specific CPU cores, clock speeds, and configurations are eagerly awaited. Qualcomm's custom Kryo cores, known for their balance between performance and power efficiency, are expected to play a crucial role in enhancing the Galaxy S24's computing capabilities.

3. Graphics Performance:

Graphics-intensive tasks, from mobile gaming to high-quality video playback, are expected to benefit from the Adreno GPU integrated into the Snapdragon 8 Gen 3. Qualcomm's GPUs have a reputation for delivering smooth and immersive graphics experiences, making the Galaxy S24 a formidable device for multimedia consumption and mobile gaming enthusiasts.

4. AI Processing:

Artificial intelligence (AI) capabilities are becoming increasingly integral to smartphones, enhancing various aspects of user experience, from camera enhancements to voice recognition. The Snapdragon 8 Gen 3 is likely to incorporate dedicated AI processing units, enabling the Galaxy S24 to execute AI-driven tasks swiftly and efficiently.

5. 5G Connectivity:

The Galaxy S24 is expected to leverage the Snapdragon 8 Gen 3's integrated 5G modem for high-speed connectivity. This ensures that users can experience the full potential of 5G networks, benefiting from faster download and upload speeds, low latency, and improved network reliability.

6. Thermal Management:

Efficient thermal management is crucial for maintaining optimal performance during prolonged usage or resource-intensive tasks. The Snapdragon 8 Gen 3 is anticipated to feature advanced thermal management mechanisms, preventing overheating and ensuring sustained peak performance for the Galaxy S24.

7. Software Optimization:

The combination of powerful hardware and optimized software is key to unlocking the full potential of a smartphone's processing power.

Samsung's One UI, layered on top of Android, is expected to be finely tuned to complement the capabilities of the Snapdragon 8 Gen 3, providing a smooth and responsive user experience on the Galaxy S24.

Processing Power: iPhone 14 Series

Apple's approach to processing power involves designing and manufacturing its custom chips, setting a benchmark for performance in the smartphone industry. The iPhone 14 Series is expected to introduce the A16 chipset, showcasing Apple's dedication to pushing the boundaries of mobile processing capabilities.

Apple's Chipset in iPhone 14 Series

1. A16 Chipset:

The A16 chipset, anticipated to power the iPhone 14 Series, is the latest iteration of Apple's custom-designed processors. Apple's A-series chips have consistently set the standard for performance and efficiency. The A16 is expected to build upon the success of its predecessors, introducing advancements in processing power, energy efficiency, and AI capabilities.

2. 5nm or Advanced Process Node:

Apple's chipsets are known for their cutting-edge manufacturing processes. The A16 is likely to be manufactured using a 5nm or more advanced process node, contributing to the chip's compact size, reduced power consumption, and enhanced overall efficiency. This enables Apple to pack more transistors into the chip, boosting computational power.

3. Neural Engine for AI:

Apple's commitment to AI is evident through the inclusion of a dedicated Neural Engine in its chipsets. The A16 is expected to feature an advanced Neural Engine, enhancing the iPhone 14's ability to execute AI-driven tasks efficiently. This includes improvements in image processing, machine learning applications, and overall device optimization based on user behavior.

4. GPU Architecture:

The graphics performance of the iPhone 14 Series is set to be driven by an updated GPU architecture integrated into the A16 chipset. Apple's GPUs have consistently delivered industry-leading graphics capabilities, ensuring a smooth and immersive experience for users engaging in graphics-intensive activities such as gaming and multimedia consumption.

5. Unified Memory Architecture:

Apple's integration of a unified memory architecture within its chipsets contributes to improved overall system performance. The A16 is likely to continue this trend, allowing the iPhone 14 to seamlessly share and access data across different components, resulting in faster data transfer and enhanced multitasking capabilities.

6. Enhanced Security Features:

Apple places a strong emphasis on user privacy and device security. The A16 chipset is expected to feature enhanced security measures, including hardware-level encryption and secure enclaves. These features contribute to a secure user experience, protecting sensitive data and ensuring the integrity of the device.

7. Integration with iOS:

The synergy between Apple's custom-designed hardware and its iOS software is a key factor in optimizing processing power. The A16 chipset and iOS are expected to be intricately integrated, ensuring that the iPhone 14 Series delivers a seamless and responsive user experience across various tasks and applications.

8. Continued Focus on Energy Efficiency:

Apple's chipsets are known not only for their raw processing power but also for their energy efficiency. The A16 is expected to continue this focus, allowing the iPhone 14 Series to deliver high performance without sacrificing battery life. This emphasis on energy efficiency is crucial for a device that aims to provide a reliable and long-lasting user experience.

In conclusion, both the Qualcomm Snapdragon 8 Gen 3 in the Galaxy S24 and Apple's A16 chipset in the iPhone 14 Series represent the forefront of mobile processing power. These chipsets, designed by industry leaders in mobile technology, are poised to deliver unparalleled performance, setting the stage for a new era of advanced and efficient smartphones. As technology continues to evolve, the processing power of these devices will play a pivotal role in shaping the user experience and pushing the boundaries of what is possible in the world of mobile computing.

CAMERA TECHNOLOGY: GALAXY S24

The camera technology in smartphones has become a central focus, shaping user preferences and driving innovations in the mobile industry. The Galaxy S24, Samsung's flagship device, is expected to introduce significant enhancements in zoom capabilities and overall camera features, solidifying its position as a leader in mobile photography.

Zoom Capabilities and Enhancements in S24

1. Advanced Optical Zoom:

Zoom capabilities are often a crucial factor in determining the versatility and quality of a smartphone camera. The Galaxy S24 is anticipated to showcase advanced optical zoom capabilities, building upon the advancements introduced in its predecessors. The introduction of periscope lenses, similar to those found in previous Samsung flagship devices, is expected to enable high levels of optical zoom without compromising image quality.

2. Hybrid Zoom Technology:

The S24 is likely to feature hybrid zoom technology, combining optical and digital zoom to provide users with a seamless and flexible zooming experience. This technology allows users to smoothly transition between different zoom levels, ensuring clarity and detail in various shooting scenarios. Samsung's commitment to refining hybrid zoom technology aims to elevate the overall zooming capabilities of the S24.

3. Computational Photography:

Samsung has been at the forefront of incorporating computational photography techniques into its camera systems. The Galaxy S24 is expected to leverage AI algorithms to enhance image processing, resulting in improved sharpness, color accuracy, and low-light performance. Computational photography not only contributes to the quality of images but also opens up creative possibilities for users.

4. Night Mode Enhancements:

Low-light photography continues to be a focal point for smartphone cameras, and the Galaxy S24 is anticipated to introduce enhancements in night mode capabilities. The combination of advanced image sensors, improved processing algorithms, and possibly larger pixel sizes is expected to result in clearer and more detailed photos in low-light conditions. Samsung's dedication to pushing the boundaries of night photography is likely to set the S24 apart in challenging lighting scenarios.

5. Pro Mode and Manual Controls:

For users with a passion for photography, the Galaxy S24 is

expected to offer Pro Mode and manual controls, allowing for a higher level of customization and creativity. Pro Mode enables users to adjust settings such as shutter speed, ISO, and focus manually, providing greater control over the photographic process. This feature caters to both enthusiasts and professional photographers seeking more advanced camera capabilities.

6. Multi-Lens Setup:

The Galaxy S24 is likely to maintain a multi-lens setup, featuring an array of lenses designed for different purposes. This may include ultra-wide-angle lenses for expansive shots, macro lenses for close-up photography, and specialized lenses for depth sensing.

The synergy of these lenses contributes to the versatility of the S24's camera system, allowing users to capture a wide range of subjects with varying perspectives.

Camera Features in iPhone 14 Series

Apple's approach to camera technology revolves around a meticulous integration of hardware and software, resulting in a cohesive and powerful camera system. The iPhone 14 Series is expected to introduce a host of camera features, building upon the success of previous iPhone models and continuing Apple's commitment to redefining mobile photography.

Camera Features in iPhone 14 Series

1. Enhanced Optical Zoom:

The iPhone 14 Series is anticipated to feature enhanced optical zoom capabilities, allowing users to get closer to their subjects without sacrificing image quality. Apple may adopt advanced lens technologies and optical zoom mechanisms to achieve higher magnification levels, catering to users who prioritize detailed and close-up shots.

2. Computational Photography Improvements:

Apple has been a trailblazer in the realm of computational photography, and the iPhone 14 Series is expected to bring further improvements in this area. The integration of advanced AI algorithms, combined with powerful hardware, is likely to result in enhanced scene recognition, better dynamic range, and improved computational processing for superior image quality.

3. AI-Driven Photography Features:

The iPhone 14 Series may introduce new AI-driven photography features, leveraging machine learning to optimize camera settings based on the recognized scene or subject. This could include intelligent scene detection, automatic adjustments for optimal exposure, and other smart enhancements that contribute to a more user-friendly and intuitive photography experience.

4. Night Mode Advances:

Low-light photography is expected to see advancements in the iPhone 14 Series, with improved Night Mode capabilities. Apple may introduce larger sensors, enhanced image signal processing, and innovative noise reduction techniques to capture clearer and more detailed photos in challenging lighting conditions. The goal is to enable users to capture stunning images even in dimly lit environments.

5. ProRAW and ProRes Video:

For users who demand professional-level control over their photography and videography, the iPhone 14 Series is anticipated to offer ProRAW for still images and ProRes video recording. ProRAW allows users to capture images in a RAW format, preserving maximum image data for post-processing flexibility. ProRes video recording, known for its high-quality compression, is expected to provide filmmakers and content creators with a powerful tool for capturing and editing high-quality videos on the go.

6. Lidar Sensor Integration:

The iPhone 14 Series is likely to continue the integration of LiDAR (Light Detection and Ranging) sensors, especially in the Pro models. LiDAR technology enhances autofocus performance in low-light conditions and contributes to the accuracy of augmented reality (AR) applications. This feature not only improves the camera's focusing capabilities but also opens up new possibilities for immersive AR experiences.

7. Multi-Lens System:

Apple's multi-lens camera system is expected to persist in the iPhone 14 Series, featuring an array of lenses with different focal lengths and purposes. This includes ultra-wide-angle lenses for expansive shots, telephoto lenses for optical zoom, and standard lenses for everyday photography. The multi-lens setup contributes to the versatility of the camera system, accommodating various shooting scenarios.

8. Deep Fusion and Smart HDR:

Deep Fusion, Apple's computational photography technology, is expected to be further refined in the iPhone 14 Series. Deep Fusion enhances image quality by leveraging machine learning to analyze and optimize pixel-level details. Smart HDR, another feature likely to see improvements, ensures optimal exposure in a variety of lighting conditions, resulting in well-balanced and vividly detailed photos.

In conclusion, both the Galaxy S24 and the iPhone 14 Series are poised to deliver groundbreaking advancements in camera technology. The competition between Samsung and Apple in this arena continues to drive innovation, offering users an unprecedented level of creativity and performance in mobile photography. As the boundaries of what is achievable with smartphone cameras expand, these flagship devices are set to redefine user expectations and usher in a new era of possibilities in the world of mobile imaging.

BATTERY LIFE: GALAXY S24

Battery life is a crucial aspect of the overall smartphone experience, impacting user satisfaction and daily usability. The Galaxy S24, Samsung's flagship device, is expected to introduce notable improvements and innovations in battery technology to ensure prolonged usage without compromising on performance.

Improvements and Innovations in S24

1. Advanced Battery Technology:

The Galaxy S24 is anticipated to feature advancements in battery technology, possibly incorporating a higher energy density battery. This improvement aims to provide users with more power in a compact form, contributing to a thinner and lighter device without sacrificing battery capacity. Samsung's commitment to staying at the forefront of battery technology aligns with the growing demand for devices that offer extended usage between charges.

2. Increased Battery Capacity:

To address the power demands of advanced features and technologies, the Galaxy S24 is likely to see an increase in battery capacity compared to its predecessors. A larger battery can provide users with more hours of screen-on time and support resource-intensive tasks, such as gaming and multimedia consumption, without requiring frequent recharging. Samsung's approach may involve optimizing the internal layout to accommodate a larger battery without significantly increasing the device's overall footprint.

3. Adaptive Battery Management:

Samsung is known for its adaptive battery management techniques, leveraging AI algorithms to optimize power consumption based on user behavior and usage patterns. The Galaxy S24 is expected to feature enhanced adaptive battery management, ensuring that power is allocated efficiently to prioritize essential tasks and background processes. This intelligent approach contributes to both improved battery life and overall device efficiency.

4. Efficient Processor Utilization:

The integration of the Qualcomm Snapdragon 8 Gen 3 processor in the Galaxy S24 plays a key role in optimizing power efficiency. The processor's advanced architecture and energy-efficient design contribute to a smoother user experience while minimizing power consumption. Samsung's collaboration with Qualcomm aims to strike a balance between high-performance capabilities and energy efficiency, ensuring that users can enjoy a responsive device without compromising on battery life.

5. Battery Optimization Across Software and Hardware:

Samsung's One UI, layered on top of Android, is expected to continue its focus on battery optimization. The seamless integration of software and hardware allows for efficient power management, minimizing background processes and optimizing system resources. The Galaxy S24 is likely to benefit from continuous refinements in both the operating system and device-specific optimizations to maximize battery efficiency.

6. Fast Charging Capabilities:

The Galaxy S24 is expected to support fast charging technologies, allowing users to quickly replenish their device's battery when needed. Samsung's proprietary fast charging solutions, possibly an evolution of previous technologies like Super Fast Charging, aim to provide a significant boost in charging speeds without compromising battery health. This feature is particularly valuable for users on the go who need a quick recharge to keep their device powered throughout the day.

7. Wireless Charging and Reverse Wireless Charging:

Continuing the trend from previous Galaxy devices, the S24 is likely to support wireless charging, offering users the convenience of cable-free charging solutions. Additionally, reverse wireless charging, a feature allowing the device to act as a wireless charging pad for other compatible devices, may be included. This innovative technology expands the utility of the device, allowing users to share power with accessories or other smartphones.

8. Battery Health Monitoring:

Samsung is expected to prioritize user awareness of battery health. The Galaxy S24 may include features and tools that enable users to monitor the condition of their battery over time. This could include insights into charging habits, battery capacity degradation, and recommendations for optimizing battery longevity. Such features contribute to a more transparent and user-centric approach to battery management.

Battery Life: iPhone 14 Series

Apple's strategy for battery life revolves around a combination of hardware optimizations, software enhancements, and a holistic approach to energy efficiency. The iPhone 14 Series is expected to continue Apple's commitment to delivering reliable and long-lasting battery performance.

Apple's Battery Strategies in iPhone 14 Series

1. Customized Battery Designs:

Apple is known for designing custom batteries tailored to each iPhone model. The iPhone 14 Series is anticipated to feature batteries designed to fit the specific dimensions of each device, maximizing capacity within the available space. This approach allows for optimized energy storage and efficient use of internal space without compromising on design or performance.

2. iOS Optimization for Battery Efficiency:

The seamless integration of iOS with Apple's custom-designed hardware plays a crucial role in optimizing battery efficiency. iOS is expected to include continuous refinements in power management algorithms, ensuring that background processes are minimized, and system resources are used judiciously. This holistic approach contributes to a responsive user experience while preserving battery life.

3. A16 Chipset's Efficiency:

The iPhone 14 Series is expected to feature Apple's latest A16 chipset, known for its efficiency and performance. The A16's advanced architecture, likely built on a 5nm or more advanced process node, contributes to improved power efficiency. The chipset's ability to deliver high performance while minimizing power consumption is a key factor in ensuring long-lasting battery life for the iPhone 14 Series.

4. Smart Battery Management:

Apple employs smart battery management strategies to enhance the overall health and longevity of iPhone batteries. This includes features such as optimized charging, which intelligently manages the charging process to reduce battery aging. The iPhone 14 Series may introduce further refinements to these smart battery management features, ensuring that users can enjoy reliable performance over the life of their devices.

5. Low Power Mode:

The iPhone 14 Series is likely to continue offering Low Power Mode, a feature that temporarily reduces background activity, visual effects, and other power-consuming processes to extend battery life when needed. This user-initiated mode is particularly useful during situations where users need to conserve battery power without sacrificing essential functionalities.

6. Improved Charging Technologies:

Apple is expected to introduce improvements in charging technologies for the iPhone 14 Series. While details are yet to be revealed, advancements in wired and wireless charging capabilities are anticipated. Apple's commitment to providing efficient and safe charging solutions aligns with the evolving standards in the industry, offering users a convenient and reliable charging experience.

7. Focus on Sustainability:

Apple places emphasis on environmental sustainability, and this extends to its approach to batteries. The iPhone 14 Series may feature batteries with recycled and responsibly sourced materials, contributing to Apple's broader initiatives to reduce its environmental impact. This sustainable

AI INTEGRATION: GALAXY AI IN SAMSUNG'S S24

Artificial Intelligence (AI) integration has become a defining feature in modern smartphones, enhancing various aspects of user experience and functionality. The Galaxy S24, Samsung's flagship device, is set to showcase the evolution of AI technology with the introduction of Galaxy AI, promising a comprehensive mobile AI experience.

Galaxy AI in Samsung's S24

1. Generative AI - Gauss:

Samsung's foray into AI was marked by the release of Gauss, a generative AI, in November. Generative AI, like

Gauss, is designed to create content, whether it's images, text, or other media, exhibiting a level of creativity and autonomy. The integration of Gauss into Galaxy AI suggests a commitment to pushing the boundaries of what AI can achieve in terms of content generation and augmentation.

2. Comprehensive Mobile AI Experience:

The description of Galaxy AI as offering a "comprehensive mobile AI experience" hints at its involvement in various aspects of the device. From optimizing battery management to enhancing camera capabilities and improving system performance, Galaxy AI is expected to be deeply integrated into the S24's ecosystem. Samsung's approach to comprehensive AI experiences aims to make the device more intuitive, responsive, and adaptive to users' needs.

3. AI-Enhanced Camera Features:

AI's role in enhancing camera features has been a notable trend, and the Galaxy S24 is likely to leverage Galaxy AI for this purpose. This could involve AI-driven scene recognition, automatic adjustments for optimal photo settings, and possibly even AI-based image post-processing. The goal is to empower users to capture high-quality images effortlessly, with the AI assisting in recognizing and optimizing camera settings based on the scene.

4. Voice Recognition and Virtual Assistant:

Voice recognition and virtual assistant capabilities are expected to be part of Galaxy AI, contributing to a more seamless user experience. Users may interact with their S24 through natural language commands, and the AI-driven virtual assistant could provide contextual information, perform tasks, and even anticipate user needs. Samsung's focus on improving voice recognition and virtual assistant functionalities aligns with the growing importance of hands-free interactions.

5. AI-Driven Personalization:

Galaxy AI is likely to play a role in personalizing the user experience. By analyzing user behavior, preferences, and usage patterns, the AI can adapt the device's settings, app suggestions, and even user interface elements to align with individual preferences. This level of personalization not only enhances user satisfaction but also showcases Samsung's commitment to making the S24 an extension of the user's personality and preferences.

6. AI in System Optimization:

AI's involvement in system optimization is crucial for delivering a smooth and responsive user experience. Galaxy AI is expected to analyze how users interact with their S24 and dynamically adjust system resources, prioritize background processes, and optimize overall performance. This level of AI-driven system optimization contributes to efficient multitasking, faster app launches, and an overall enhanced user experience.

7. Integration with Samsung Services:

Galaxy AI is likely to integrate with Samsung's ecosystem of services, creating a cohesive and interconnected user experience. From health and fitness tracking to smart home control, the AI's integration with various Samsung services aims to provide users with a centralized hub for managing different aspects of their digital life. This approach aligns with Samsung's strategy of offering a seamless and integrated ecosystem of devices and services.

8. Continuous Learning and Adaptation:

One of the key characteristics of advanced AI systems is their ability to continuously learn and adapt. Galaxy AI is expected to evolve over time based on user interactions, feedback, and emerging trends. This continuous learning approach ensures that the S24 remains at the forefront of AI technology, adapting to changing user needs and preferences.

Apple's AI Capabilities in iPhone 14 Series

Apple's approach to AI integration revolves around creating a cohesive and intelligent user experience while prioritizing user privacy. The iPhone 14 Series is expected to build upon Apple's existing AI capabilities, incorporating advancements in machine learning, natural language processing, and contextual understanding.

Apple's AI Capabilities in iPhone 14 Series

1. Siri - Apple's Virtual Assistant:

Siri, Apple's virtual assistant, is a cornerstone of the company's AI capabilities. With each iteration, Siri becomes more adept at understanding natural language commands, providing relevant information, and performing tasks. The iPhone 14 Series is likely to introduce improvements in Siri's capabilities, enhancing its ability to interact contextually and assist users in their daily tasks.

2. On-Device Machine Learning:

Apple emphasizes on-device machine learning, ensuring that sensitive user data stays on the device rather than being sent to the cloud. This approach enhances user privacy while allowing the device to leverage machine learning for tasks such as predictive text, image recognition, and personalization. The iPhone 14's AI capabilities are expected to showcase advancements in on-device machine learning, enabling faster and more accurate AI-driven functionalities.

3. Advanced Camera AI:

The iPhone 14 Series is anticipated to feature advancements in AI-driven camera capabilities. This could include improved scene recognition, enhanced portrait mode, and intelligent adjustments based on the photographed subjects. Apple's dedication to refining camera AI aligns with the growing importance of photography in smartphone usage, aiming to deliver a camera system that is not only powerful but also smart and intuitive.

4. AI-Enhanced Personalization:

Apple's AI capabilities contribute to the personalization of the iPhone experience. The iPhone 14 Series is likely to analyze user behavior, app usage patterns, and preferences to offer personalized suggestions, recommendations, and shortcuts. This level of personalization ensures that the device adapts to individual users, making it a more intuitive and user-centric tool.

5. Privacy-Focused AI:

Apple's commitment to user privacy extends to its AI strategies. The iPhone

14's AI capabilities are expected to prioritize user data protection, employing techniques like differential privacy to gather insights without compromising individual privacy. This approach distinguishes Apple in the industry, resonating with users who value data security and privacy.

6. Augmented Reality (AR) Integration:

Apple has been a pioneer in integrating AI with augmented reality (AR). The iPhone 14 Series is likely to introduce further advancements in AR capabilities, leveraging AI for improved object recognition, spatial awareness, and interactive AR experiences. The synergy between AI and AR enhances the iPhone's capabilities beyond traditional smartphone functionalities.

7. Enhanced Predictive Capabilities:

Apple's AI capabilities contribute to the device's predictive features, anticipating user needs and preferences. Whether it's predictive text, app suggestions, or contextual shortcuts, the iPhone 14 is expected to showcase improvements in predictive capabilities. This level of intelligence ensures that the device becomes more proactive in assisting users, streamlining their interactions and workflows.

8. Continuous Improvement Through Updates:

Apple's commitment to providing regular software updates ensures that the AI capabilities of the iPhone 14 Series continue to evolve. As new machine learning models and algorithms are developed, Apple can seamlessly introduce these advancements through software updates, keeping the device at the forefront of AI technology even after its initial release.

In conclusion, both the Galaxy S24 with Galaxy AI and the iPhone 14 Series with Apple's AI capabilities represent the latest strides in incorporating artificial intelligence into the smartphone experience. While Samsung aims to offer a comprehensive AI ecosystem, Apple emphasizes a privacy-focused approach, both contributing to an increasingly intelligent, personalized, and user-friendly interaction with smartphones. As AI continues to play a central role in shaping the future of mobile technology, these devices showcase

DISPLAY AND MULTIMEDIA: Screen Technology in Galaxy S24

The display technology of a smartphone is a pivotal factor in determining the overall user experience, especially in the context of multimedia consumption, gaming, and daily interactions. The Galaxy S24, Samsung's flagship device, is poised to showcase cutting-edge screen technology, further elevating the standard for vibrant visuals and immersive multimedia experiences.

Screen Technology in Galaxy S24

1. Dynamic AMOLED Display:

Samsung is renowned for its vibrant and high-quality AMOLED displays, and the Galaxy S24 is expected to continue this legacy with a Dynamic AMOLED screen. This display technology allows for individual pixel control, resulting in deep blacks, vibrant colors, and high contrast ratios. The Dynamic AMOLED display is likely to offer HDR support, contributing to a visually stunning experience when viewing HDR content.

2. High Refresh Rate:

To enhance the overall fluidity and responsiveness of the user interface, the Galaxy S24 is anticipated to feature a high refresh rate display. A refresh rate of 120Hz or higher ensures smoother animations, reduced motion blur, and a more responsive touch experience. This feature is particularly beneficial for gaming and navigating through the device's interface with precision.

3. Quad HD+ Resolution:

Samsung's flagship devices often boast Quad HD+ resolution, providing a high pixel density for crisp and detailed visuals. The Galaxy S24 is expected to continue this trend, offering users a sharp and clear display for various activities, including reading, video streaming, and photo viewing. The combination of high resolution and AMOLED technology contributes to an immersive viewing experience.

4. Under-Display Camera Technology:

Innovations in display technology may extend to the integration of an under-display camera in the Galaxy S24. This technology allows the front-facing camera to be hidden beneath the display, providing a seamless and uninterrupted screen surface. While details about the implementation remain speculative, the inclusion of under-display camera technology aligns with Samsung's pursuit of maximizing the screen-to-body ratio.

5. S-Pen Support:

The Galaxy S24 may continue Samsung's tradition of S-Pen support, offering users the flexibility to take notes, sketch, and navigate the device with precision. The integration of S-Pen support complements the display technology by providing users with a versatile input method, expanding the possibilities for creativity and productivity.

6. Eye Comfort Features:

Samsung is likely to incorporate eye comfort features into the Galaxy S24's display, including blue light filters and adaptive brightness. These features aim to reduce eye strain during prolonged usage, making the device more comfortable for reading or extended multimedia consumption, especially in low-light conditions.

7. Dolby Atmos Audio:

Multimedia experiences on the Galaxy S24 extend beyond the display, with Dolby Atmos audio enhancing the audio quality. The combination of high-quality visuals and immersive sound contributes to a cinematic experience when watching movies, playing games, or streaming content. Samsung's commitment to delivering a comprehensive multimedia experience is evident in the integration of Dolby Atmos technology.

8. Enhanced Multitasking Capabilities:

The Galaxy S24's display is expected to support enhanced multitasking capabilities, possibly through features like split-screen or pop-up view. The large and high-resolution display provides users with ample screen real estate to run multiple apps simultaneously, fostering productivity and convenience for users who multitask frequently.

9. Adaptive Display Technology:

Samsung's adaptive display technology is designed to automatically adjust the screen settings based on the surrounding environment and user preferences. This includes dynamic adjustments to color temperature, contrast, and brightness. The Galaxy S24 is likely to feature advancements in adaptive display technology, ensuring optimal visibility and comfort in various lighting conditions.

Advancements in Display for iPhone 14 Series

Apple's approach to display technology centers around delivering a visually pleasing and color-accurate experience while prioritizing factors such as True Tone, ProMotion technology, and the integration of high-quality materials. The iPhone 14 Series is expected to introduce advancements in display technology, aligning with Apple's commitment to providing a premium and immersive user experience.

Advancements in Display for iPhone 14 Series

1. ProMotion Technology:

The iPhone 14 Series is anticipated to feature ProMotion technology, which allows for a high refresh rate display. This feature ensures a smoother and more responsive user experience by dynamically adjusting the display's refresh rate based on the content being viewed. ProMotion is particularly beneficial for tasks such as scrolling, gaming, and overall navigation.

2. Advanced True Tone:

True Tone, a feature introduced by Apple, is likely to see advancements in the iPhone 14 Series. True Tone dynamically adjusts the white balance of the display to match the ambient lighting conditions, providing a more natural and comfortable viewing experience. Enhancements in True

Tone technology contribute to more accurate color representation and improved readability.

3. Pro Display XDR Technology:

The iPhone 14 Pro models may inherit display technologies from Apple's Pro Display XDR, the high-end display used in professional settings. This could include improvements in contrast ratios, color accuracy, and peak brightness. The integration of Pro Display XDR technology aims to bring a level of visual fidelity to the iPhone 14 Pro Series that appeals to users who prioritize professional-grade display capabilities.

4. OLED or MicroLED Display:

Apple may continue its transition to more advanced display technologies, with the iPhone 14 Series potentially adopting OLED or even MicroLED displays. These technologies offer advantages such as improved power efficiency, higher contrast ratios, and better color accuracy. The choice between OLED and MicroLED will likely depend on factors such as production feasibility and overall performance goals.

5. Improved Screen-to-Body Ratio:

Advancements in display technology often contribute to improvements in the screen-to-body ratio of smartphones. The iPhone 14 Series is expected to continue the trend of minimizing bezels and maximizing the display area, providing users with a more immersive visual experience. The increased screen-to-body ratio enhances the aesthetic appeal of the device and contributes to a modern design.

6. Adaptive HDR:

HDR (High Dynamic Range) support is integral to delivering vibrant and lifelike visuals. The iPhone 14 Series may introduce adaptive HDR technology, dynamically adjusting HDR settings based on the content being viewed. This ensures that users experience optimal HDR performance across a variety of supported media, from videos and photos to gaming content.

7. Enhanced Color Accuracy:

Apple's commitment to color accuracy is likely to manifest in the iPhone 14 Series with advancements in color calibration and representation. A display with enhanced color accuracy ensures that users experience content as intended by content creators, whether it's viewing photos, videos, or other multimedia content.

8. ProRAW and ProRes Display Support:

If the iPhone 14 Series introduces ProRAW for still images and ProRes video recording, the display technology is expected to support these advanced formats. ProRAW images, with their uncompressed and unprocessed data, would benefit from a display capable of showcasing intricate details. Similarly, ProRes video playback would demand a high-quality display to deliver the intended visual experience.

9. Spatial Audio Integration:

Spatial Audio, a feature that provides an immersive audio experience, may contribute to the overall multimedia experience on the iPhone 14 Series. The integration of spatial audio technology aligns with Apple's emphasis on creating a holistic and sensory-rich environment for users engaging with multimedia content on their devices.

In conclusion, both the Galaxy S24 and the iPhone 14 Series are poised to deliver advancements in display technology that enhance the overall user experience.

CONNECTIVITY AND FEATURES: 5G Capabilities and Connectivity Options

The realm of smartphones is continually evolving, with connectivity being a key focus area for manufacturers. The Galaxy S24 and iPhone 14 Series are anticipated to be at the forefront of this evolution, offering advanced 5G capabilities and a range of connectivity options to ensure users stay connected seamlessly.

5G Capabilities

1. 5G Network Support:

Both the Galaxy S24 and the iPhone 14 Series are expected to embrace the next-generation 5G connectivity, delivering faster download and upload speeds, lower latency, and improved overall network performance. The integration of 5G support aligns with the global rollout of 5G networks, enabling users to experience enhanced connectivity for data-intensive tasks, such as streaming high-definition content and real-time online activities.

2. Sub-6GHz and mmWave Support:

To provide comprehensive 5G coverage, these flagship devices are likely to support both Sub-6GHz and mmWave frequency bands. Sub-6GHz offers broader coverage, making it suitable for urban and suburban areas, while mmWave provides ultra-fast speeds in denser urban environments.

The dual-support approach ensures users can access 5G networks across a variety of geographic locations.

3. Improved Network Efficiency:

The adoption of 5G brings not only faster speeds but also improved network efficiency. Both the Galaxy S24 and iPhone 14 Series are expected to leverage 5G technologies to enhance the efficiency of data transfer, resulting in a more responsive and fluid online experience. This efficiency is crucial for applications like cloud-based services, real-time gaming, and augmented reality (AR) experiences.

4. Enhanced Streaming and Downloading:

5G capabilities significantly impact streaming and downloading experiences. With faster download speeds, users can seamlessly stream high-definition content without buffering delays, and large files can be downloaded in a fraction of the time compared to previous generations of networks. The integration of 5G ensures that users can enjoy a more immersive and uninterrupted multimedia experience on their devices.

5. Low Latency for Real-Time Applications:

Low latency is a hallmark of 5G networks, making real-time applications and services more responsive. Both the Galaxy S24 and iPhone 14 Series are expected to benefit from reduced latency, enhancing the performance of applications like online gaming, video conferencing, and AR applications. The lower latency ensures a more natural and seamless user experience in these real-time scenarios.

6. Global 5G Roaming:

As 5G networks expand globally, users increasingly demand seamless connectivity when traveling. The Galaxy S24 and iPhone 14 Series are likely to support global 5G roaming, allowing users to access high-speed networks in different countries without the need for complex configurations. This feature is particularly valuable for business travelers and users who frequently move between regions.

Connectivity Options

1. Wi-Fi 6E Support:

Wi-Fi 6E, an extension of Wi-Fi 6, operates in the 6GHz frequency band, providing additional spectrum for improved performance. Both flagship devices are expected to support Wi-Fi 6E, offering faster data transfer speeds, reduced congestion, and enhanced reliability for Wi-Fi connectivity. This is especially beneficial in scenarios where users rely on Wi-Fi networks for high-bandwidth activities.

2. Bluetooth 5.2:

The Galaxy S24 and iPhone 14 Series are likely to feature Bluetooth 5.2 support, bringing improvements in data transfer speeds, range, and overall connectivity reliability. Bluetooth 5.2 introduces advancements like enhanced audio quality with support for multiple audio streams, making it ideal for wireless audio accessories and multitasking scenarios.

3. NFC for Contactless Payments:

Near Field Communication (NFC) technology is a staple for contactless payments, and both devices are expected to continue supporting NFC. This enables users to make secure and convenient payments using mobile wallet services, such as Samsung Pay and Apple Pay. The ubiquity of NFC ensures compatibility with a wide range of payment terminals and other NFC-enabled devices.

4. USB Type-C Connectivity:

USB Type-C has become the standard for wired connectivity, offering fast data transfer speeds and versatile usage. The Galaxy S24 and iPhone 14 Series are likely to feature USB Type-C ports for charging, data transfer, and connecting to various accessories. The universal nature of USB Type-C ensures compatibility with a diverse range of peripherals.

5. Dual SIM and eSIM Support:

Dual SIM functionality allows users to use two SIM cards simultaneously, providing flexibility in managing personal and business contacts or utilizing local and international plans. Both devices are expected to support dual SIM capabilities, with one of the SIM slots likely to be an eSIM. eSIM technology enables remote SIM provisioning, simplifying the process of activating a new mobile plan without a physical SIM card.

6. Advanced Location Services:

Both the Galaxy S24 and iPhone 14 Series are expected to feature advanced location services, leveraging technologies like GPS, GLONASS, and Galileo for precise location tracking.

This is crucial for applications ranging from navigation and fitness tracking to location-based services and augmented reality experiences.

Unique Features in Galaxy S24 and iPhone 14 Series

Galaxy S24:

1. Under-Display Camera Technology:

The Galaxy S24 is rumored to feature under-display camera technology, providing users with a nearly bezel-less display by concealing the front-facing camera beneath the screen. This innovative approach enhances the device's aesthetics while maintaining the functionality of the front camera.

2. S-Pen Integration:

Building on Samsung's legacy, the Galaxy S24 may continue to support the S-Pen, offering users a versatile stylus for note-taking, drawing, and navigating the device. The integration of the S-Pen enhances the device's productivity and creative capabilities.

3. Galaxy AI:

Galaxy AI, with its generative AI capabilities introduced through Gauss, is expected to play a prominent role in the Galaxy S24. From camera enhancements to system optimizations, Galaxy AI aims to deliver a comprehensive and intelligent user experience.

MARKET POSITIONING: Comparative Sales and Market Share

The market positioning of smartphones is a dynamic landscape shaped by competitive forces, consumer preferences, and technological advancements. Both the Galaxy S24 and iPhone 14 Series are set to make significant impacts in the smartphone market, each bringing its unique strengths and appealing to distinct consumer segments.

Comparative Sales and Market Share

1. Historical Sales Trends:

Examining historical sales trends provides valuable insights into the market positioning of both the Galaxy S series and the iPhone. Samsung's Galaxy S series has established itself as a strong competitor, with consistent sales performance across various models. On the other hand, Apple's iPhone series has consistently dominated the premium smartphone market, enjoying a loyal customer base and strong sales figures.

2. Global Market Share:

The global market share of Samsung and Apple in the smartphone industry is a critical indicator of their respective market positions. Historically, Samsung has been a major player, often competing neck-and-neck with

Apple. Market share is influenced by factors such as device affordability, regional preferences, and brand loyalty, making it a key metric for assessing the competitive landscape.

3. Regional Variances:

Market positioning is not uniform across regions, and analyzing regional variances in sales and market share provides a nuanced perspective. In some regions, Samsung's Galaxy S series may outperform the iPhone, while in others, Apple's ecosystem and brand appeal might lead to higher sales. Understanding regional dynamics is crucial for both manufacturers to tailor their strategies to local consumer preferences.

4. Emerging Markets vs. Established Markets:

The market positioning of the Galaxy S24 and iPhone 14 Series will be influenced by their performance in both emerging and established markets. In emerging markets, factors such as affordability, feature-rich offerings, and brand recognition play a pivotal role. Established markets often focus on premium features, cutting-edge technology, and brand prestige. Striking a balance between these market demands is essential for sustained success.

5. Impact of Mid-Range and Budget Models:

The smartphone market is not solely defined by flagship models, as mid-range and budget devices contribute significantly to overall sales. Samsung has a diverse lineup that includes a range of devices catering to different price points. Apple, while traditionally focusing on premium devices, has introduced more budget-friendly options in recent years. The impact of mid-range and budget models on overall sales and market share will influence the market positioning of both manufacturers.

6. Competitive Landscape with Other Brands:

Beyond the Galaxy S series and iPhone, the competitive landscape includes a multitude of smartphone manufacturers. Brands like Huawei, Xiaomi, and OnePlus vie for market share, introducing innovative features and competitive pricing. Understanding how the Galaxy S24 and iPhone 14 Series navigate this crowded space is crucial for assessing their overall market positioning.

7. Brand Loyalty and Retention:

Brand loyalty plays a significant role in market positioning, especially in the smartphone industry where users often stick to a particular brand. Apple has cultivated a strong sense of brand loyalty, with many iPhone users upgrading to newer models within the Apple ecosystem. Samsung, with its diverse product range, aims to retain existing customers while attracting new ones through technological innovations.

8. Impact of Supply Chain Challenges:

Global supply chain challenges, such as semiconductor shortages and manufacturing delays, have ripple effects on sales and market share. Both Samsung and Apple face the complexities of navigating these challenges, and how they manage supply chain disruptions will influence their ability to meet consumer demand, impacting market positioning.

CONSUMER PREFERENCES AND TRENDS

1. Camera and Imaging Capabilities:

Consumer preferences in recent years have shown a strong inclination towards smartphones with advanced camera capabilities. Features like high megapixel counts, multiple lenses for versatile photography, and AI-driven enhancements are significant factors. The Galaxy S24 and iPhone 14 Series are expected to prioritize camera technology to align with this trend, offering users powerful imaging capabilities.

2. 5G Connectivity:

The advent of 5G networks has sparked interest among consumers, driving preferences towards devices with 5G capabilities. Both Samsung and Apple recognize the importance of

5G connectivity, and the Galaxy S24 and iPhone 14 Series are expected to leverage this trend by providing enhanced network speeds and low latency, catering to users who prioritize cutting-edge connectivity.

3. Display Technology and Size:

Large, high-resolution displays with vibrant colors and high refresh rates continue to be a key preference among consumers. The Galaxy S24 and iPhone 14 Series are likely to feature advancements in display technology, including improvements in resolution, refresh rates, and possibly new form factors. Consumer preferences for immersive multimedia experiences and expansive displays will influence the market positioning of these devices.

4. Ecosystem Integration:

The integration of smartphones within broader ecosystems, including smartwatches, tablets, and smart home devices, is gaining prominence. Apple's ecosystem, centered around seamless integration with other Apple products, has been a significant driver of consumer loyalty. Samsung's Galaxy ecosystem is also expanding, and the success of the Galaxy S24 will be influenced by its ability to integrate seamlessly with other Samsung devices.

5. Sustainability and Environmental Considerations:

Consumer preferences are increasingly leaning towards environmentally sustainable products. Both Samsung and Apple have made commitments to sustainability, with initiatives such as using recycled materials in device construction and reducing electronic waste. Consumer awareness of environmental considerations may influence the market positioning of the Galaxy S24 and iPhone 14 Series.

6. Biometric Security and Privacy Features:

Biometric security features, including facial recognition and fingerprint scanning, are crucial elements of consumer preferences. Additionally, privacy features that prioritize user data protection are gaining significance. The Galaxy S24 and iPhone 14 Series are expected to enhance biometric security and privacy features to align with evolving consumer expectations in these areas.

7. Software Updates and Long-Term Support:

Consumers value timely software updates and long-term support for their devices. Apple has been known for providing consistent software updates across its device lineup, contributing to prolonged device longevity. Samsung has also made strides in this area with its commitment to regular updates. Consumer preferences for devices with extended software support will impact the market positioning of both the Galaxy S24 and iPhone 14 Series.

8. Gaming and Performance:

The gaming capabilities of smartphones continue to influence consumer preferences, especially among the younger demographic. Both manufacturers are likely to focus on delivering high-performance devices, with advanced processors, graphics capabilities, and features specifically tailored for gaming experiences. The success of the Galaxy S24 and iPhone